I0020112

Your Guide to Fixing a Slow Computer

**Easy DIY Solutions to Speed Up Your PC
By Upgrading Hardware, Cleaning Out
Clutter, Optimizing Internet Connectivity,
and Preventing Future Lag Issues**

Savvy Quick Fix Joel

Copyright © 2023 by Savvy Quick Fix Joel

All rights reserved. No part of this publication may be reproduced, distributed, or transmitted in any form or by any means, including photocopying, recording, or other electronic or mechanical methods, without the prior written permission of the publisher, except in the case of brief quotations embodied in critical reviews and certain other noncommercial uses permitted by copyright law.

This book is a work of non-fiction. Names, characters, businesses, organizations, places, events, and incidents either are the product of the author's imagination or are used fictitiously. Any resemblance to actual persons, living or dead, events, or locales is entirely coincidental.

Table of Contents

Introduction

Have you ever experienced the frustration of a slow, lagging computer that seems to have a mind of its own, refusing to keep up with your demands? Perhaps you've found yourself amid a critical task, only to be thwarted by the spinning wheel of doom or the hourglass of endless waiting. If so, you're not alone. We've all been there, teetering on the edge of technological exasperation, wondering if there's a way to breathe new life into our sluggish machines.

In the fast-paced world we navigate, a slow computer isn't just an inconvenience; it's a roadblock, a hindrance to productivity, and a source of genuine stress. We get it, the frustration, the impatience, the yearning for a seamless computing experience. But fear not, for within the pages of this guide, a revelation awaits, a comprehensive roadmap to transform your computer from a sluggish burden to a nimble ally.

As we embark on this journey together, we will delve deep into the core struggles that make your computer a reluctant companion. From hardware limitations to the chaos of cluttered software, we'll unravel the mysteries that contribute to your computer's lethargy. But that's not all – we won't just stop at understanding the pain points;

we're here to provide you with practical, DIY solutions that empower you to take control.

Imagine a world where your computer responds swiftly to your every command, where lag is but a distant memory. Picture the joy of seamless multitasking, the relief of instant startup, and the satisfaction of a system optimized to its full potential. This guide is your ticket to that reality.

By the time you reach the final page, you'll not only have conquered the obstacles slowing down your computer, but you'll also emerge with newfound expertise. Better gas mileage? Consider it done. Saving money? Absolutely. Contributing to a healthier environment? You'll be pleasantly surprised.

So, dear reader, are you ready to bid farewell to the sluggish woes of your computer and usher in an era of peak performance? The solutions await, and your journey to a faster, more efficient computing experience starts now. Let's turn frustration into triumph together!

Chapter 1

Understanding the Causes of Slow Performance

Hardware Bottlenecks

In the digital realm, speed is the name of the game. Your computer, once a swift companion, might now be dragging its feet, leaving you in the dust. Let's unpack why this happens, starting with the often elusive culprits known as hardware bottlenecks.

Hardware Bottlenecks
Have you ever felt like your computer's running shoes suddenly turned into heavy boots? That's the hardware bottleneck, an invisible force holding your system back.*

Identifying the Culprit:
First, take a moment to picture your computer as a team of athletes passing a baton in a relay race. The baton represents data, and each athlete is a component of your hardware, CPU, RAM, storage, and graphics card. When one athlete slows down, the entire team suffers. That's the bottleneck effect.

Common Bottlenecks:

1. Outdated CPU:
- An old, sluggish CPU can't keep up with modern software demands.
- Upgrading to a faster processor can breathe new life into your system.

2. Insufficient RAM:
- Imagine trying to juggle too many balls at once, that's what insufficient RAM feels like.
- Adding more RAM allows your computer to handle multiple tasks effortlessly.

3. Slow Storage Drives:
- Think of your storage drive as the locker where your data hangs out. Slow drives mean slow access.
- Upgrading to a solid-state drive (SSD) can significantly boost speed.

What You Can Do:

1. Assess Your Hardware:
- First, identify the weak link, is it the CPU, RAM, or storage?
- Use system monitoring tools to track performance.

2. Upgrade Strategically:

- Depending on your budget and needs, prioritize upgrading the bottlenecked component.
- Upgrades don't have to break the bank; they just need to target the right area.

Recap:

Understanding hardware bottlenecks is like diagnosing a performance athlete's stumbling block. Identify the weak link, invest strategically in upgrades, and watch your computer sprint past the competition.

Software Issues

Now that we've peeled back the layers of hardware bottlenecks, let's dive into the shadowy realm of software issues. Your computer might not be weighed down by physical limitations, but a cluttered digital landscape can slow it down just as much.

Imagine your computer as a sleek sports car navigating a winding road. Now, picture that road cluttered with potholes and detours, that's what software issues do to your system's performance.

The Stealthy Culprits:

1. Background Processes:
- Behind the scenes, countless processes run, hogging resources.
- Identify and trim down unnecessary background applications.

2. Fragmented Hard Drives:
- Think of a fragmented hard drive as a messy bookshelf, it takes longer to find what you need.
- Regularly defragmenting your hard drive organizes data for faster access.

3. Unoptimized Software:
- Not all software is created equal; some are resource hogs.
- Opt for lightweight alternatives or optimize settings for efficiency.

Taking Action:

1. Task Manager is Your Ally:
- Open your Task Manager (Ctrl + Shift + Esc) to see what's consuming resources.
- End unnecessary tasks and processes to free up your computer's power.

2. Regular Maintenance:
- Set up a schedule for software updates, ensuring you have the latest versions.
- Remove unused applications, a digital declutter can do wonders.

3. Optimize Startup Programs:
- Picture your computer's startup as a race, the faster it sprints off the blocks, the quicker you get to work.
- Disable unnecessary startup programs for a swifter launch.

What You Can Do:

1. Digital Spring Cleaning:
- Regularly go through your installed programs and uninstall those you don't use.
- Clear out temporary files and caches to free up valuable space.

2. Smart Software Choices:
- Before downloading, research software for efficiency and user reviews.
- Consider alternative programs that offer the same functionality without the bloat.

Recap:
Software issues are the hidden roadblocks in your computer's journey to peak performance. Keep an eye on resource-hungry processes, maintain your software diligently, and choose your digital companions wisely for a smoother ride.

Internet Connectivity Problems

As we untangle the web of your computer's slow performance, it's crucial to explore the often-overlooked realm of internet connectivity problems. Your computer's speed isn't just about its internal components; it's also about how seamlessly it dances with the online world.*

Internet Connectivity Problems

Picture this: your computer is a skilled performer on a grand stage, but if the stage is shaky, the performance suffers. That's what happens when internet connectivity issues take center stage.

The Invisible Hurdles:

1. Slow Network Speeds:
- Slow internet is like trying to run a marathon through waist-deep mud.
- Check your internet plan, and if possible, upgrade for faster speeds.

2. Wi-Fi Interference:
- Imagine your Wi-Fi signals as radio stations, interference disrupts the signal.
- Position your router strategically and avoid electronic devices that could cause interference.

3. Outdated Network Drivers:
- Think of network drivers as traffic police, outdated ones lead to chaos.
- Regularly update your network drivers for smoother data flow.

Troubleshooting Steps:

1. Speed Test Reality Check:
- Use online speed tests to measure your actual internet speed.
- If it falls below your subscribed speed, contact your internet service provider.

2. Router Optimization:
- Ensure your router firmware is up-to-date.
- Experiment with different Wi-Fi channels to find the least congested one.

3. Driver Update Protocol:
- Navigate to Device Manager, find your network adapter, and update its drivers.
- Consider using the manufacturer's website for the latest driver version.

What You Can Do:

1. Internet Health Check:
- Regularly monitor your internet speed and contact your provider if it consistently underperforms.
- Educate yourself on troubleshooting common Wi-Fi issues.

2. Router TLC:
- Treat your router with care place it in a central location, away from obstructions.
- Secure your Wi-Fi network with a strong password to prevent unauthorized usage.

Recap:
Internet connectivity problems are the silent saboteurs of your computer's performance. Regularly assess your internet speed, optimize your router's settings, and stay vigilant against interference for a smoother online experience.

In the next section, we'll explore how to assess your computer's overall performance and identify patterns of lag, bringing us one step closer to a swift and efficient system.

Chapter 2

Assessing Your Computer's Performance

Performance Monitoring Tools

Now that we've uncovered the potential hurdles your computer faces, it's time to put on the detective hat. In this chapter, we'll delve into the world of performance assessment, arming you with the tools and know-how to diagnose and cure your computer's laggy tendencies.

Performance Monitoring Tools
Imagine your computer as a patient, and performance monitoring tools as the diagnostic instruments in a doctor's office. These tools unveil the inner workings of your system, allowing us to pinpoint areas of concern.

The Power of Insight:

1. Task Manager:
First on our list is the ever-reliable Task Manager (Ctrl + Shift + Esc). It's like an x-ray, showing you which processes are consuming resources.

Action Step: Regularly check Task Manager to identify resource-hungry applications and end unnecessary processes.

2. Resource Monitor:
Resource Monitor offers a deeper dive, akin to a full-body scan. It provides real-time data on CPU, memory, disk, and network usage.
Action Step: Use Resource Monitor to identify specific processes causing bottlenecks and address them.

3. Performance Monitor (PerfMon):
Think of PerfMon as your computer's fitness tracker. It records performance over time, helping you spot trends and anomalies.
Action Step: Set up custom performance counters to track specific metrics, aiding in proactive troubleshooting.

Putting Tools to Work:

1. Identify Resource Hogs:
As you navigate through Task Manager and Resource Monitor, look for processes with high CPU or memory usage.
Action Step: Address resource-hogging applications by closing or uninstalling them.

2. Monitor Trends:

In PerfMon, observe performance metrics over days or weeks. Look for patterns of lag during specific activities. **Action Step:** Use trend analysis to anticipate and mitigate potential performance issues.

3. Benchmarking Tools:

Benchmarking tools act as performance referees, comparing your system against industry standards. **Action Step:** Run benchmark tests to assess your computer's performance relative to its capabilities.

What You Can Do:

1. Regular Check-ups:

Schedule routine performance checks using these tools. **Action Step:** Make performance assessment a regular part of your computer maintenance routine.

2. Customize Alerts:

Set up alerts in PerfMon for critical performance thresholds. **Action Step:** Receive notifications when certain metrics exceed predefined limits.

Recap:

Performance monitoring tools are your diagnostic allies, providing insights into your computer's health. Regularly use Task Manager, Resource Monitor, and PerfMon to identify and address resource hogs, monitor trends, and keep your system in peak condition.

In the upcoming chapters, we'll dive into actionable strategies to upgrade your hardware, declutter your system, and optimize internet connectivity, all aimed at transforming your computer into a high-performance powerhouse.

Identifying Lag Patterns

Now that we've equipped you with the tools to monitor your computer's performance, it's time to become a performance detective. In this section, we'll explore the art of identifying lag patterns, recognizing when and why your computer hits a speed bump.

Identifying Lag Patterns

Imagine your computer as a skilled dancer, and lag as an awkward stumble during a routine. By understanding the patterns of these stumbles, you can choreograph a smoother, more graceful performance.

Observing Lag Patterns:

1. Activity-Specific Lag:

Picture this: You're editing photos, and suddenly your computer hesitates. Recognizing activity-specific lag is crucial.

Action Step: Note when lag occurs, during gaming, editing, or multitasking.

2. Time of Day Trends:

Just as traffic varies throughout the day, so can your computer's performance. Recognize peak usage times.

Action Step: Log instances of lag and check if they coincide with high-demand periods.

3. Consistency vs. Random Spikes:
Is lag a constant companion or an occasional nuisance? Understanding consistency helps pinpoint root causes.

Action Step: Differentiate between consistent, chronic lag and sporadic, random spikes.

Diagnosing Lag Causes:

1. Resource-Specific Lag:
If lag is tied to a specific resource (CPU, RAM, disk), it points to a bottleneck in that area.

Action Step: Review performance monitoring tools to identify the resource under stress.

2. Software-Induced Lag:
Some software applications may be more lag-prone. Identify if certain programs consistently trigger slowdowns.

Action Step: Experiment with alternative programs or optimize settings.

3. Network-Related Lag:

Lag during online activities? It might be a network issue. Recognizing the source is key to a targeted solution.

Action Step: Run internet speed tests during laggy periods to identify network-related problems.

What You Can Do:

1. Keep a Lag Journal:

Maintain a log noting when lag occurs, what activities you were engaged in, and any common factors.

Action Step: Use the lag journal as a reference when troubleshooting.

2. Test in Controlled Environments:

Isolate your computer's usage to specific tasks during testing to pinpoint lag triggers.

Action Step: Identify if lag is consistent across various activities or tied to specific tasks.

Recap:

Identifying lag patterns is akin to decoding a performance language. Observe when lag strikes, note the patterns, and diagnose the root causes. Armed with this knowledge, you're ready to implement targeted solutions in the upcoming chapters.

Next, we'll dive into actionable strategies to upgrade your hardware, starting with a focus on your computer's beating heart, the Central Processing Unit (CPU).

Chapter 3

Upgrading Hardware for Better Performance

RAM Upgrade Strategies

As we embark on the journey to revitalize your computer's performance, hardware upgrades are the key to unleashing its full potential. In this chapter, we'll start with a spotlight on one of the primary architects of speed, your computer's Random Access Memory (RAM). Let's explore actionable strategies to breathe new life into your system.

RAM Upgrade Strategies

Think of RAM as your computer's workspace, the more available, the smoother it operates. Upgrading your RAM is like expanding your office, allowing your computer to juggle more tasks without breaking a sweat.

Understanding RAM's Role:

1. Temporary Storage Powerhouse:
RAM is your computer's short-term memory, holding data that the CPU actively uses.
Action Step: Imagine a desk, RAM is the space where your computer works on its current tasks.

2. Multitasking Muscle:
Ever opened too many tabs and felt your computer slow down? That's a RAM limitation.
Action Step: Consider RAM as your computer's ability to juggle multiple tasks simultaneously.

Choosing the Right RAM:

1. DDR4 vs. DDR3:
RAM comes in different generations. DDR4 is faster and more efficient than DDR3.
Action Step: Check your motherboard compatibility and opt for DDR4 if possible.

2. Capacity Matters:
8GB might have been sufficient, but with modern applications, consider upgrading to 16GB or more.
Action Step: Assess your current RAM usage and choose a capacity that accommodates your needs.

Installation Process:

1. Locate RAM Slots:
Open your computer case and identify available RAM slots on the motherboard.
Action Step: Consult your motherboard manual or online resources for slot locations.

2. Anti-Static Precautions:
Before handling RAM, discharge static electricity by touching a grounded metal object.
Action Step: Avoid damaging components by practicing anti-static measures.

3. Align and Seat Firmly:
Position the RAM module correctly in the slot and press down until the clips lock into place.
Action Step: Confirm secure installation by gently pushing down on the sides of the RAM module.

Post-Upgrade Testing:

1. Boot and Check BIOS:
Turn on your computer and enter the BIOS to confirm the system recognizes the new RAM.
Action Step: Ensure the correct RAM capacity and speed are detected.

2. Performance Verification:

Run performance tests or engage in typical multitasking to witness the enhanced speed.

Action Step: Revel in the newfound responsiveness of your upgraded RAM.

Recap:

Upgrading your RAM is like giving your computer a turbo boost. Understand its role, choose the right RAM specifications, follow a careful installation process, and bask in the performance gains. In the next section, we'll explore upgrading another crucial hardware component – your storage solution. Get ready to usher in a new era of speed!

Choosing the Right Storage Solution

In the quest for a swifter computer, our attention now turns to another vital component, the storage solution. Upgrading your storage can significantly impact not only speed but also the overall responsiveness of your system. In this section, we'll unravel the intricacies of choosing the right storage solution for your needs.

Choosing the Right Storage Solution
Think of your storage solution as the filing cabinet of your computer, where data is stored for quick retrieval. Upgrading this component is akin to replacing an old, creaky filing system with a state-of-the-art, high-speed repository.

Understanding Storage Types:

1. Hard Disk Drives (HDDs):
Traditional HDDs are like classic filing cabinets, reliable but not the speediest.
Action Step: Consider HDDs for mass storage where speed is not a primary concern.

2. Solid-State Drives (SSDs):
SSDs are the speed demons of storage solutions, lightning-fast data access.

Action Step: Opt for SSDs for your operating system, frequently used applications, and critical files.

Key Factors in Choosing:

1. Capacity vs. Speed:
Balance your need for storage space with the desire for speed. SSDs offer faster performance but at a higher cost per gigabyte.
Action Step: Consider a combination of SSD for speed-critical tasks and HDD for mass storage.

2. Form Factor:
Ensure the physical size of the storage device (2.5-inch or M.2 for SSDs, 3.5-inch for HDDs) fits your computer's specifications.
Action Step: Check your computer's compatibility and available slots for the chosen form factor.

3. Connection Interface:
Different storage devices use various interfaces (SATA, PCIe). Choose one compatible with your motherboard.
Action Step: Confirm the interface your motherboard supports before purchasing.

Installation Process:

1. Cloning or Fresh Install:
When upgrading to an SSD, decide whether to clone your existing drive or perform a fresh installation.
Action Step: Cloning retains your data but might not fully capitalize on the SSD's potential.

2. Data Migration:
Transfer your files and operating system to the new drive using migration software.
Action Step: Follow step-by-step guides for data migration to ensure a seamless transition.

Post-Upgrade Benefits:

1. Faster Boot Times:
Experience swift startup times as your operating system loads from the high-speed SSD.
Action Step: Delight in the quick responsiveness of your upgraded storage.

2. Speedier Application Launch:
Applications installed on an SSD launch almost instantly, reducing wait times.
Action Step: Enjoy a seamless computing experience with rapid application responsiveness.

Recap:

Choosing the right storage solution involves balancing capacity and speed, considering form factors and connection interfaces, and navigating the installation process. Whether opting for the speed of SSDs or the mass storage of HDDs, upgrading your storage solution will undoubtedly enhance your computer's overall performance. Next up, we'll delve into graphics card enhancements, unlocking a realm of possibilities for gaming, content creation, and beyond!*

Graphics Card Enhancements

Now, let's venture into the realm of graphics card enhancements, a key player in elevating your computer's visual experience. Whether you're a gamer, content creator, or just seeking smoother graphics, upgrading your graphics card can be a game-changer.

Graphics Card Enhancements
Think of your graphics card as the artist behind the canvas, rendering vibrant images and ensuring smooth video playback. Upgrading this component opens the door to a world of visual delight and enhanced performance.

Understanding Graphics Cards:

1. Integrated vs. Dedicated Graphics:
Integrated graphics share resources with your computer's main processor, suitable for basic tasks. Dedicated graphics cards, on the other hand, have dedicated memory and processing power, ideal for demanding applications.
Action Step: Assess your needs, dedicated graphics for gaming, content creation, or graphics-intensive tasks.

2. GPU (Graphics Processing Unit):

The GPU is the powerhouse of the graphics card, handling complex calculations for rendering images and videos.

Action Step: Look for a graphics card with a powerful GPU for smoother performance in graphics-intensive applications.

Choosing the Right Graphics Card:

1. Performance vs. Budget:

Graphics cards come in a range of performance levels and prices. Consider your budget and the performance you need.

Action Step: Research benchmark scores and reviews to find the best balance for your requirements.

2. Compatibility:

Ensure your chosen graphics card is compatible with your motherboard and power supply.

Action Step: Check the physical size of the graphics card, available PCIe slots, and power supply requirements.

Installation Process:

1. Driver Installation:
Before physically installing the graphics card, download the latest drivers from the manufacturer's website.
Action Step: Install the drivers for optimal performance and stability.

2. Physical Installation:
Power off your computer, remove the side panel and insert the graphics card into the appropriate PCIe slot.
Action Step: Secure the card in place, ensuring it clicks into the slot, and connect the required power cables.

Post-Upgrade Benefits:

1. Enhanced Gaming Experience:
Enjoy smoother gameplay, higher frame rates, and better graphics details with an upgraded graphics card.*
Action Step: Dive into your favorite games and witness the difference.

2. Improved Content Creation:
Accelerate video rendering, 3D modeling, and graphic design tasks with a powerful graphics card.
Action Step: Experience faster rendering times and a more responsive workflow.

Recap:

Graphics card enhancements are a gateway to a visually stunning and high-performance computing experience. Consider your specific needs, balance performance with your budget, and ensure compatibility before installation. With a new graphics card, you're not just upgrading visuals; you're unlocking the potential for an entirely new level of computing. In the next section, we'll delve into strategies for cleaning out clutter and optimizing your system for peak performance.

Chapter 4

Cleaning Out Clutter

Disk Cleanup and Organization

Now that we've upgraded key hardware components, it's time to address the digital clutter bogging down your system. In this chapter, we'll explore strategies for efficient disk cleanup and organization, a crucial step toward achieving a streamlined and responsive computer.

Disk Cleanup and Organization

Imagine your computer's storage as a tidy workspace, clutter-free, well-organized, and ready for optimal performance. Disk cleanup and organization are the digital equivalents of decluttering your desk.

Understanding Digital Clutter:

1. Temporary Files and Caches:

Over time, your computer accumulates temporary files and caches, taking up valuable storage space.

Action Step: Regularly sweep away these files to keep your storage lean.

2. Unused Applications:

Unused applications can be digital dust, occupying space without contributing to your computing experience.

Action Step: Identify and uninstall applications that no longer serve a purpose.

Efficient Disk Cleanup:

1. Built-In Tools:

Windows and macOS come equipped with built-in disk cleanup tools.

Action Step: Utilize tools like Disk Cleanup (Windows) or Disk Utility (macOS) to remove unnecessary files.

2. Third-Party Cleanup Utilities:

Explore third-party applications that offer advanced cleaning features.

Action Step: CCleaner, for instance, can help identify and remove junk files with precision.

Organizing Your Digital Space:

1. Folder Structure:

Organize your files into logical folders for easy access and efficient management.

Action Step: Create folders for documents, images, videos, and other file types.

2. Desktop Decluttering:
A cluttered desktop can slow down your system's performance.
Action Step: Keep the desktop tidy by moving files into categorized folders.

Optimizing Disk Space:

1. Storage Analysis:
Use storage analysis tools to identify space-hogging files and folders.
Action Step: Address large files or folders that contribute to storage bloat.

2. Cloud Storage Solutions:
Consider offloading files to cloud storage to free up local storage space.
Action Step: Utilize services like Google Drive, Dropbox, or OneDrive for seamless file synchronization.

Regular Maintenance Routine:

1. Scheduled Cleanup:
Make disk cleanup and organization a part of your regular maintenance routine.
Action Step: Set reminders or schedule automated cleanup tasks for convenience.

2. Backup Your Data:
Before performing major cleanup operations, ensure your critical data is backed up.
Action Step: Use external drives or cloud backups for added security.

Recap:
Disk cleanup and organization are essential for maintaining a nimble and efficient computer. Regularly purge unnecessary files, create an organized file structure, and optimize your disk space for peak performance. In the upcoming sections, we'll delve into optimizing internet connectivity and enhancing your system's overall performance.

Managing Startup Programs

In the ongoing quest for a faster and more responsive computer, managing startup programs is a critical aspect of decluttering. In this section, we'll unravel the significance of controlling what launches with your computer, ensuring a swift and focused startup experience.

Managing Startup Programs
Think of your computer's startup as a grand entrance – the smoother and faster, the better. Managing startup programs is like curating a guest list, allowing only essential attendees for a streamlined and efficient beginning.

Understanding Startup Programs:

1. Automatic Launch on Boot:
Some applications set themselves to launch automatically when you start your computer.
Action Step: Identify and manage these startup programs to optimize boot times.

2. Impact on Boot Speed:
The more programs launching at startup, the longer it takes for your computer to become fully operational.

Action Step: Streamline the startup process by allowing only necessary programs to launch.

Efficient Startup Management:

1. Task Manager (Windows) or Activity Monitor (macOS):
Both Windows and macOS provide tools to manage startup programs.
Action Step: Open Task Manager (Ctrl + Shift + Esc) on Windows or Activity Monitor on macOS to view and control startup items.

2. Startup Tab (Windows) or Login Items (macOS):
Windows users can navigate to the "Startup" tab in Task Manager, while macOS users can access "Login Items" in System Preferences.
Action Step: Review and disable unnecessary programs set to launch at startup.

Identifying Unnecessary Startup Programs:

1. Ask Yourself: "Is It Essential?":
Consider the necessity of each program that launches at startup.
Action Step: Disable programs that aren't crucial for immediate use.

2. Impact on System Resources:

Some startup programs consume valuable system resources even after booting.

Action Step: Disable resource-heavy programs to ensure a responsive system.

Optimizing Boot Times:

1. Prioritize Essential Programs:

Ensure critical applications like antivirus software and system utilities are allowed to launch at startup.

Action Step: Prioritize security and essential system tools in your startup list.

2. Regular Review:

As you install new software, periodically review and adjust your startup programs.

Action Step: Stay proactive by regularly revisiting and optimizing your startup list.

Recap:

Managing startup programs is an impactful strategy for decluttering your computer and optimizing its boot times. Use built-in tools like Task Manager or Activity Monitor, ask critical questions about program necessity, and regularly review and adjust your startup list. In the next section, we'll explore fine-tuning your internet connectivity for a seamless online experience.

Uninstalling Unnecessary Software

In the pursuit of a lean and responsive computer, uninstalling unnecessary software is a pivotal step. This section delves into the art of decluttering your system by identifying and removing programs that no longer serve a purpose.

Uninstalling Unnecessary Software
Consider your computer as a well-organized library, each software application is a book contributing to its functionality. Uninstalling unnecessary software is akin to clearing out outdated books to make room for new, essential additions.

Understanding Unnecessary Software:

1. Unused and Outdated Programs:
Over time, you accumulate software that may have served a purpose once but is now obsolete or redundant.
Action Step: Identify programs that you no longer use or need.

2. Resource-Heavy Applications:
Some applications may consume substantial system resources without providing proportional value.
Action Step: Evaluate the impact of each application on your computer's performance.

Efficient Uninstallation Process:

1. Programs and Features (Windows) or Applications (macOS):
Access the "Programs and Features" menu on Windows or "Applications" on macOS to view installed software.
Action Step: Review the list and identify programs for uninstallation.

2. Use Official Uninstaller (if available):
Some programs come with dedicated uninstallers provided by the software developer.
Action Step: Check the program's documentation or official website for uninstallation instructions.

Identifying Unnecessary Software:

1. Evaluate Program Usage:
Ask yourself how frequently you use each installed program.
Action Step: Uninstall programs that are rarely or never used.

2. Check for Alternatives:
Explore whether there are alternative programs that serve the same purpose more efficiently.
Action Step: Replace outdated or resource-heavy programs with more optimized alternatives.

Optimizing System Performance:

1. Frequent Review:
Make uninstalling unnecessary software a routine practice to maintain a clutter-free system.
Action Step: Set a schedule to review installed programs and remove any that are no longer essential.

2. Disk Cleanup After Uninstallation:
After uninstalling the software, run disk cleanup tools to remove residual files.
Action Step: Ensure that all remnants of uninstalled programs are cleared for maximum efficiency.

Recap:
Uninstalling unnecessary software is akin to decluttering your computer's software library. Regularly assess your installed programs, remove unused or outdated ones, and optimize your system for peak performance. The next section will delve into strategies for optimizing internet connectivity, ensuring a seamless online experience.

Chapter 5

Optimizing Internet Connectivity

Troubleshooting Network Issues

As we continue our journey to unlock the full potential of your computer, the focus now shifts to optimizing internet connectivity. In this chapter, we'll explore effective strategies for troubleshooting network issues, ensuring a seamless online experience.

Troubleshooting Network Issues

Imagine your computer as a high-speed race car navigating a digital highway. To ensure it zips through without hiccups, we need to troubleshoot and eliminate any roadblocks hindering your internet connectivity.

Understanding Network Issues:

1. Inconsistent Speeds:

Internet speeds can vary, impacting your ability to stream, download, or engage in online activities.

Action Step: Identify and resolve inconsistencies in your internet speed.

2. Intermittent Connectivity:

Frequent drops in internet connectivity can disrupt online tasks and cause frustration.

Action Step: Investigate and address issues causing intermittent connectivity.

Efficient Troubleshooting:

1. Speed Test:

Use online speed tests to measure your internet speed and compare it to your subscribed plan.

Action Step: Conduct regular speed tests to ensure your provider delivers the promised speeds.

2. Router Placement:

The location of your router can impact signal strength and overall connectivity.

Action Step: Place your router centrally and elevate it to reduce interference and improve coverage.

3. Check for Interference:

Electronic devices and neighboring networks can interfere with your Wi-Fi signal.

Action Step: Identify and eliminate sources of interference for a stable connection.

Isolating Connectivity Issues:

1. Device-Specific Tests:
Check if the connectivity issue is specific to one device or affecting multiple devices.
Action Step: Run tests on different devices to pinpoint the source of the problem.

2. Router Reboot:
Sometimes, a simple router reboot can resolve connectivity issues.
Action Step: Power cycle your router by unplugging it, waiting a minute, and plugging it back in.

Advanced Troubleshooting:

1. Update Router Firmware:
Outdated router firmware can contribute to network issues.
Action Step: Visit the router manufacturer's website and update firmware following their instructions.

2. Contact Internet Service Provider (ISP):
If issues persist, reach out to your ISP to address potential problems on their end.
Action Step: Communicate speed test results and connectivity issues for further assistance.

Optimizing Wi-Fi Security:

1. Secure Your Wi-Fi Network:
Unsecured networks invite unauthorized usage and may lead to performance issues.
Action Step: Enable WPA3 encryption and set a strong password for your Wi-Fi network.

2. Manage Connected Devices:
The number of connected devices can strain your network.
Action Step: Monitor and manage connected devices, ensuring they aren't overwhelming your bandwidth.

Recap:
Troubleshooting network issues is essential for maintaining a stable and efficient internet connection. From basic tests to advanced troubleshooting, the goal is to identify and resolve issues affecting your online experience. In the next section, we'll explore strategies for enhancing overall system performance.*

Wi-Fi and Ethernet Optimization Tips

In the pursuit of an optimal online experience, the focus now turns to Wi-Fi and Ethernet optimization. This chapter explores practical tips to fine-tune both wireless and wired connections, ensuring a seamless and efficient internet experience.

Wi-Fi and Ethernet Optimization Tips

Imagine your internet connection as a well-tuned orchestra, each instrument (device) playing in harmony to deliver a smooth and consistent performance. Let's delve into strategies to optimize both Wi-Fi and Ethernet connections.

Wi-Fi Optimization Tips:

1. Choose the Right Wi-Fi Channel:

Wi-Fi routers operate on different channels, and interference can arise if multiple routers use the same channel.

Action Step: Use a Wi-Fi analyzer tool to identify less congested channels and set your router accordingly.

2. Optimal Router Placement:

Router placement affects signal strength. Centralize your router and avoid obstacles like walls and electronic devices.

Action Step: Elevate the router and place it in a central location for better coverage.

3. Update Router Firmware:
Router manufacturers release firmware updates to address bugs and enhance performance.
Action Step: Regularly check for and install the latest firmware updates for your router.

4. Use Quality of Service (QoS) Settings:
QoS settings prioritize certain types of internet traffic, ensuring a smoother experience for critical applications.
Action Step: Configure QoS settings to prioritize activities like online gaming or video streaming.

5. Implement Wi-Fi Security Measures:
Securing your Wi-Fi network prevents unauthorized access and ensures optimal performance.
Action Step: Enable WPA3 encryption and set a strong password to protect your Wi-Fi network.

Ethernet Optimization Tips:

1. Check Cable Quality:
Ethernet cables come in various categories. Ensure you're using high-quality cables that support your internet speed.

Action Step: Upgrade to Cat6 or Cat6a cables for faster and more reliable connections.

2. Avoid Cable Interference:
Ethernet cables can be affected by interference from power lines or electronic devices.
Action Step: Keep Ethernet cables away from sources of interference for optimal performance.

3. Update Network Drivers:
Outdated network drivers can impact Ethernet performance.
Action Step: Regularly update network drivers for your computer's network adapter.

4. Check Router and Switch Performance:
Routers and switches play a crucial role in Ethernet connections. Ensure they can handle your internet speed.
Action Step: Upgrade to a gigabit router or switch if needed for faster data transfer.

5. Utilize Quality Ethernet Ports:
Connect your devices to high-quality Ethernet ports for optimal performance.
Action Step: Prioritize gigabit Ethernet ports over slower alternatives when connecting devices.

Hybrid Tips for Both Wi-Fi and Ethernet:

1. Restart Your Router:
A simple router restart can refresh connections and resolve temporary issues.
Action Step: Periodically restart your router for optimal performance.

2. Regular Network Health Checks:
Monitor your network health using diagnostic tools to identify and address potential issues proactively.
Action Step: Use built-in network diagnostic tools or third-party applications to assess your network's health.

Recap:
Optimizing both Wi-Fi and Ethernet connections involves a combination of smart settings, proper equipment, and routine maintenance. Whether you're navigating the wireless spectrum or embracing the reliability of wired connections, these tips will contribute to a well-orchestrated internet experience. In the next section, we'll explore strategies for enhancing your system's overall performance.

Updating Network Drivers

Within the realm of internet optimization, ensuring that your network drivers are up-to-date is a crucial step towards a smoother online experience.

Updating Network Drivers
Imagine your network drivers as the conductors orchestrating the flow of data between your device and the vast digital landscape. Keeping them up-to-date ensures a harmonious symphony of connectivity.

Understanding Network Drivers:

1. Essential Communication Bridge:
Network drivers act as translators, facilitating communication between your operating system and network hardware.
Action Step: Regular updates enhance compatibility and performance.

2. Impact on Connectivity and Speed:
Outdated network drivers can lead to connectivity issues, slower internet speeds, and potential security vulnerabilities.
Action Step: Keep drivers current to benefit from performance improvements and security patches.

Effective Driver Update Process:

1. Identify Your Network Adapter:
Determine the manufacturer and model of your network adapter.
Action Step: Check the device manager on Windows or system information on macOS to find details about your network adapter.

2. Visit the Manufacturer's Website:
Navigate to the official website of your network adapter's manufacturer.
Action Step: Locate the support or download section and search for the latest drivers for your specific model.

3. Download the Latest Drivers:
Download the most recent version of the network drivers compatible with your operating system.
Action Step: Ensure compatibility by choosing the correct driver version for your OS (Windows, macOS, Linux).

4. Backup Existing Drivers (Optional):
Consider backing up your current network drivers before updating.
Action Step: Use built-in tools or third-party software to create a backup in case issues arise.

5. Uninstall Old Drivers:
Before installing the new drivers, uninstall the existing ones to avoid conflicts.
Action Step: Access the device manager, right-click on your network adapter, and select "Uninstall device."

6. Install New Drivers:
Execute the downloaded driver installer and follow the on-screen instructions.
Action Step: Reboot your computer if prompted, ensuring the changes take effect.

Benefits of Updated Network Drivers:

1. Improved Performance:
Updated drivers often include performance optimizations, resulting in a faster and more stable connection.
Action Step: Experience enhanced internet speeds and smoother online activities.

2. Enhanced Compatibility:
Compatibility with the latest software and protocols ensures a seamless online experience.
Action Step: Stay current to avoid potential issues with newer applications and technologies.

3. Security Patches:
Updated drivers often include security patches, protecting your system from potential vulnerabilities.
Action Step: Ensure a more secure online environment by keeping drivers up-to-date.

Scheduled Driver Checks:

1. Set Reminders for Regular Checks:
Make updating network drivers a routine task to ensure ongoing performance improvements.
Action Step: Set calendar reminders or utilize automatic update tools for regular checks.

2. Monitor Manufacturer Communications:
Stay informed about driver updates by subscribing to newsletters or checking the manufacturer's communication channels.
Action Step: Manufacturers often release updates in response to evolving technologies and user feedback.

Recap:
Updating network drivers is a fundamental practice to maintain optimal internet connectivity. By following a systematic approach to identify, download, and install the latest drivers, you contribute to a more reliable and efficient online experience.

Chapter 6

Enhancing System Performance

System Tweaks and Settings

As we delve deeper into the realm of system optimization, this chapter explores invaluable strategies for enhancing your computer's overall performance. System tweaks and settings adjustments act as the maestros, fine-tuning your system to achieve peak efficiency.

System Tweaks and Settings

Consider your computer as a finely tuned instrument, each tweak and adjustment contributes to the symphony of optimal performance. Let's unravel the key system tweaks and settings to elevate your computing experience.

Understanding System Tweaks:

1. Power Plan Optimization:

Power plans dictate how your computer manages energy consumption.

Action Step: Customize power plans to balance performance and energy efficiency based on your usage.

2. Visual Effects:
Graphics and animation effects contribute to the visual appeal but may impact system performance.
Action Step: Adjust visual effects settings to find the right balance between aesthetics and performance.

3. Virtual Memory Settings:
Virtual memory is a space on your hard drive used as an extension of physical RAM.
Action Step: Optimize virtual memory settings to ensure efficient memory management.

Efficient System Settings:

1. Startup and Recovery Settings:
Fine-tune startup and recovery settings for a streamlined boot process and efficient error handling.
Action Step: Customize startup options and error reporting settings in system properties.

2. System Restore:
System Restore allows you to revert your system to a previous state in case of issues.
Action Step: Configure System Restore settings to manage disk space and frequency of restore points.

3. Windows Search Indexing:

Indexing speeds up file searches but can impact system resources.

Action Step: Adjust Windows Search indexing settings to optimize performance.

Advanced System Tweaks:

1. Registry Optimizations:

The Windows Registry stores system settings and configurations.

Action Step: Exercise caution and make informed changes to the registry for advanced optimizations.

2. Processor Scheduling:

Customize processor scheduling to prioritize foreground applications for smoother performance.

Action Step: Adjust processor scheduling settings in system properties.

System Maintenance:

1. Disk Cleanup and Defragmentation:

Regular disk cleanup and defragmentation ensure efficient use of storage space and faster file access.

Action Step: Schedule periodic disk cleanup and defragmentation tasks for optimal performance.

2. Windows Updates:
Keep your operating system up-to-date with the latest security patches and performance improvements.
Action Step: Enable automatic Windows updates or regularly check for and install updates.

Performance Monitoring:

1. Task Manager Insights:
Task Manager provides real-time insights into system resource usage.
Action Step: Monitor Task Manager regularly to identify resource-hungry processes and applications.

2. Third-Party Performance Tools:
Explore third-party performance monitoring tools for in-depth analysis.
Action Step: Use tools like HWMonitor or Speccy to gather detailed performance metrics.

Recap:
System tweaks and settings adjustments are the keys to unlocking your computer's full potential. From power plans to advanced registry optimizations, each tweak contributes to a finely tuned system. Regular maintenance, performance monitoring, and staying informed about system updates ensure a consistently optimized computing experience.

Registry Cleanup and Maintenance

In our journey towards optimal system performance, one area that demands careful attention is the Windows Registry. This section unravels the intricacies of Registry cleanup and maintenance, providing insights and guidelines for a well-maintained and responsive computing environment.

Registry Cleanup and Maintenance

Think of the Windows Registry as the backstage organizer, storing critical settings and configurations for your operating system and applications. Maintaining this registry ensures a smoothly orchestrated performance.*

Understanding the Windows Registry:

1. Registry's Role:

The Registry stores information about system hardware, software settings, user preferences, and more.

Action Step: Recognize the significance of a healthy and well-maintained Registry for overall system stability.

2. Registry Hives:

The Registry is organized into hives, each containing specific types of information.

Action Step: Understand the structure of Registry hives, including

HKEY_CLASSES_ROOT, HKEY_CURRENT_USER, HKEY_LOCAL_MACHINE, and others.

When to Consider Cleanup:

1. Excessive Entries:
Over time, the Registry may accumulate unnecessary or obsolete entries, potentially affecting system performance.
Action Step: Consider cleanup when troubleshooting issues or optimizing system performance.

2. After Software Uninstallations:
Some applications may leave remnants in the Registry after uninstallation.
Action Step: Perform Registry cleanup after uninstalling software to remove lingering entries.

Registry Cleanup Tools:

1. Registry Editor (Regedit):
The built-in Registry Editor allows manual inspection and modification of the Registry.
Action Step: Exercise caution and make informed changes using Regedit.

2. Third-Party Registry Cleaners:
Various third-party tools automate the cleanup process, scanning for and removing unnecessary entries.

Action Step: Use reputable Registry cleaners cautiously, as improper use may cause issues.

Safe Registry Cleanup Practices:

1. Backup Before Making Changes:
Create a backup or restore point before making any Registry changes.

Action Step: This ensures you can revert to a previous state in case of unintended issues.

2. Focus on Redundant Entries:
Identify and remove redundant or orphaned Registry entries that serve no purpose.

Action Step: Take time to research entries before deletion to avoid unintended consequences.

Registry Maintenance:

1. Regular Checkups:
Perform periodic checks to identify and address Registry issues proactively.

Action Step: Schedule routine inspections using tools like System File Checker (SFC) to ensure Registry health.

2. Avoid Unnecessary Changes:

Make changes only when necessary, and avoid modifying Registry entries without a clear understanding of their impact.

Action Step: Stick to well-documented tweaks and modifications to minimize risks.

Advanced Considerations:

1. Fragmentation:

Registry fragmentation can occur, potentially impacting performance.

Action Step: Advanced users may explore tools specifically designed for defragmenting the Registry.

2. Unused Class IDs (CLSID):

Remove unused CLSIDs associated with uninstalled software.

Action Step: Use caution and consult reliable sources before deleting CLSIDs.

Recap:

Registry cleanup and maintenance are integral components of ensuring a responsive and stable computing environment. Whether manually using Registry Editor or employing third-party tools, approach cleanup with caution, prioritize backups, and stay informed about the changes you make. With a well-maintained Registry, your system is poised for optimal performance. In the subsequent section, we'll address preventive measures to safeguard against future lag issues.

Power Settings for Efficiency

In the pursuit of an efficient and responsive computer, the optimization journey extends to power settings. This section explores the intricacies of power settings and how fine-tuning them can significantly impact the balance between performance and energy conservation.

Power Settings for Efficiency
Imagine your computer's power settings as the conductor orchestrating the energy flow within your system. By optimizing these settings, you can strike the perfect harmony between performance and power conservation.

Understanding Power Plans:

1. Power Plans Overview:
Power plans are pre-configured sets of hardware and system settings that manage how your computer uses power.
Action Step: Familiarize yourself with the available power plans on your operating system, typically including Balanced, High Performance, and Power Saver.

2. Balancing Act:
Different power plans strike different balances between performance and energy conservation.

Action Step: Choose a power plan that aligns with your usage patterns, balancing performance needs with energy efficiency.

Customizing Power Plans:

1. Create a Custom Power Plan:
Tailor a power plan to your specific preferences by creating a custom plan.
Action Step: Adjust settings such as screen brightness, sleep mode duration, and CPU performance to align with your needs.

2. Processor Power Management:
Fine-tune how your processor operates under varying workloads.
Action Step: Adjust minimum and maximum processor states to optimize performance and conserve power.

Power Plan Optimization Tips:

1. Adaptive Brightness:
Enable adaptive brightness to automatically adjust screen brightness based on ambient light conditions.
Action Step: This not only enhances visibility but also contributes to energy conservation.

2. Sleep and Hibernate Settings:
Configure sleep and hibernate settings to strike a balance between responsiveness and power savings.
Action Step: Set appropriate durations for sleep and hibernate modes to suit your usage patterns.

Advanced Power Options:

1. Hard Disk Power Management:
Manage hard disk power to balance energy conservation and performance.
Action Step: Adjust settings to spin down the hard disk after a specific period of inactivity.

2. USB Selective Suspend:
Enable USB Selective Suspend to save power by selectively turning off USB ports.
Action Step: This is particularly useful for portable devices, extending battery life on laptops.

Power Efficiency and Laptops:

1. Battery Saver Mode:
Activate Battery Saver mode on laptops to maximize battery life.
Action Step: This mode often limits background processes and adjusts system settings for energy efficiency.

2. Graphics Settings:

Configure graphics settings to balance performance and power consumption on laptops with dedicated GPUs.

Action Step: Choose between integrated and dedicated graphics based on your current usage.

Regular Power Plan Assessment:

1. Review and Adjust Regularly:

Regularly reassess your power plan settings based on your evolving usage patterns.

Action Step: Adjust settings to match your current needs, especially when transitioning between tasks.

2. Dynamic Switching (Hybrid Graphics):

Laptops with hybrid graphics can dynamically switch between integrated and dedicated GPUs based on workload.

Action Step: Optimize settings to allow for seamless transitions between graphics options.

Recap:

Power settings play a pivotal role in defining the balance between system performance and energy conservation. By understanding and customizing power plans to align with your needs, you can optimize your computer's efficiency. Whether you're focused on maximizing performance or conserving battery life on a laptop, these power settings are crucial tools in your optimization toolkit. In the upcoming section, we'll explore preventive measures to ensure a lag-free computing experience in the future.

Chapter 7

Preventing Future Lag Issues

Best Practices for Regular Maintenance

As we navigate the path towards a seamlessly performing computer, the focus now shifts to proactive measures aimed at preventing future lag issues. This chapter outlines best practices for regular maintenance, emphasizes the importance of antivirus and malware protection, and underscores the significance of automatic updates and patch management.

Best Practices for Regular Maintenance
Imagine regular maintenance as the routine care that keeps your computer in top shape, preventing potential lags and slowdowns.

Scheduled Disk Cleanup and Defragmentation:

1. Disk Cleanup:
Regularly rid your system of unnecessary files, freeing up valuable storage space.

Action Step: Use the built-in Disk Cleanup tool to remove temporary files, system cache, and other clutter.

2. Disk Defragmentation:
Optimize file placement on your hard drive to enhance read and write speeds.
Action Step: Schedule periodic defragmentation, or rely on automatic optimization tools.

Regular Software Updates:

1. Operating System Updates:
Keep your operating system up-to-date to benefit from performance enhancements and security patches.
Action Step: Enable automatic updates or regularly check for and install updates.

2. Application Updates:
Update third-party applications to access new features, bug fixes, and improved performance.
Action Step: Utilize automatic updates where available, or set reminders to check for updates regularly.

Temporary Files Management:

1. Browser Cache and Cookies:
Periodically clear your browser's cache and cookies to maintain efficient browsing speeds.

Action Step: Explore browser settings to clear cache and cookies, or use browser extensions for automated cleanup.

2. Temporary Files:
Regularly clear temporary files generated by the system and applications.
Action Step: Utilize disk cleanup tools or third-party applications to streamline this process.

Hardware Health Check:

1. Temperature Monitoring:
Monitor your system's temperature to prevent overheating and potential performance throttling.
Action Step: Use temperature monitoring tools to ensure hardware operates within safe ranges.

2. Dust and Debris Removal:
Dust buildup can impact cooling efficiency. Periodically clean internal components.
Action Step: Safely clean dust and debris from fans, vents, and heat sinks.

Antivirus and Malware Protection

Choosing a Reliable Antivirus Solution:

1. Real-Time Protection:
Select an antivirus program that offers real-time protection against viruses and malware.
Action Step: Enable real-time scanning to detect and neutralize threats as they emerge.

2. Regular Scans:
Schedule regular system scans to identify and eliminate potential threats.
Action Step: Configure automatic scans during periods of low system usage.

Safe Browsing Habits:

1. Email Vigilance:
Exercise caution with email attachments and links, common vectors for malware.
Action Step: Avoid opening attachments or clicking on links from unknown or suspicious sources.

2. Secure Websites:
Ensure websites use secure connections, especially when sharing sensitive information.
Action Step: Look for "https://" in the URL and check for security indicators in your browser

Automatic Updates and Patch Management

Keeping your software and operating system updated with the latest patches is a crucial defense against vulnerabilities. This section emphasizes the significance of automatic updates and effective patch management.

Automatic Updates:

1. Operating System Updates:

Enable automatic updates for your operating system to receive critical security patches.

Action Step: Configure settings to automatically download and install updates.

2. Application Updates:

Utilize automatic updates for applications to ensure you're running the latest, most secure versions.

Action Step: Enable automatic updates within application settings or use built-in updaters.

Patch Management Best Practices:

1. Timely Patch Installation:

Install patches promptly to close vulnerabilities and bolster your system's security.

Action Step: Regularly check for patches and apply them as soon as they are available.

2. Patch Testing:
Before applying patches, test them in a controlled environment to ensure compatibility and avoid unforeseen issues.

Action Step: Establish a test environment to assess the impact of patches before widespread deployment.

Recap:
Preventing future lag issues involves a proactive approach to regular maintenance, robust antivirus and malware protection, and diligent management of automatic updates and patches. By incorporating these best practices into your computing routine, you not only optimize performance but also safeguard your system against potential threats and vulnerabilities. In the next section, we'll explore strategies for troubleshooting common issues and fine-tuning your system for peak efficiency.

Conclusion

Congratulations! You've embarked on a journey to transform your computer into a powerhouse of efficiency and reliability. From diagnosing the causes of slow performance to implementing hardware upgrades, cleaning out clutter, optimizing internet connectivity, and mastering system tweaks, you've gained a toolkit for unparalleled performance.

But our exploration doesn't end here. By embracing power settings for efficiency, undertaking regular maintenance, fortifying your defense with antivirus measures, and staying vigilant with automatic updates, you've fortified your system against lag issues and potential threats.

As you implement these strategies, remember that a well-tuned computer isn't just a machine; it's a gateway to seamless productivity, immersive entertainment, and stress-free computing. Embrace the joy of a responsive system, liberated from the shackles of lag.

Your journey towards a lag-free computing experience doesn't stop here. Continue to stay informed, adapt to emerging technologies, and revel in the enhanced performance of your rejuvenated computer. Here's to a future of uninterrupted computing bliss!

www.ingramcontent.com/pod-product-compliance
Lightning Source LLC
Chambersburg PA
CBHW071306050326
40690CB00011B/2542